NDHI ALBERT EINSTEIN

SA JOHN FITZGERALD KENNEDY ANWAR

IESEL MARTIN LUTHER KING, JR.

GARI MAATHAI AUNG SAN SUU KYI

MAHATMA GANDHI ALBERT EINSTEIN

MOTHER TERESA JOHN FITZGERALD

AVEZ ELIE WIESEL MARTIN LUTHER

WANGARI MAATHAI AUNG SAN SUU KYI

N MAHATMA GANDHI ALBERT EINSTEIN

MOTHER TERESA JOHN FITZGERALD

AVEZ ELI MARTIN LUTHER

WANGARI SAN SUU KYI

MAHAT ERT EINSTEIN

MOTHER FITZGERALD

ELIE W UTHER KING

ANGARI M SAN SUU KYI

MAHAT ERT EINSTEIN

MOTHE FITZGERALD

AVEZ EL RTIN LUTHER

WANGARI SAN SUU KYI

ERSON HI ALBERT

H BUNCH RESA JOHN

CESAR CH EL MARTIN

LAI LAMA WANGARI MAATHAI AUNG

ALDO EMERSON MAHATMA GANDHI

RALPH WALDO EMERSON ❦ MAHATMA
GANDHI ❦ ALBERT EINSTEIN ❦ ELEANO
ROOSEVELT ❦ RALPH BUNCHE ❦ MOTHE
TERESA ❦ JOHN FITZGERALD KENNEDY ❦
ANWAR EL-SADAT ❦ CESAR CHAVEZ ❦ ELI
WIESEL ❦ MARTIN LUTHER KING, JR.
❦ ANNE FRANK ❦ THE DALAI LAMA ❦
WANGARI MAATHAI ❦ AUNG SAN SUU KYI ❦
PRINCESS DIANA ❦ RALPH WALDO EMERSO
❦ MAHATMA GANDHI ❦ ALBERT EINSTEIN ❦
ELEANOR ROOSEVELT ❦ RALPH BUNCH
❦ MOTHER TERESA ❦ JOHN FITZGERAL
KENNEDY ❦ ANWAR EL-SADAT ❦ CESA
CHAVEZ ❦ ELIE WIESEL ❦ MARTIN LUTHE
KING, JR. ❦ ANNE FRANK ❦ THE DALA
LAMA ❦ WANGARI MAATHAI ❦ AUNG SA
SUU KYI ❦ PRINCESS DIANA ❦ RALP
WALDO EMERSON ❦ MAHATMA GANDHI ❦
ALBERT EINSTEIN ❦ ELEANOR ROOSEVEL
❦ RALPH BUNCHE ❦ MOTHER TERESA ❦
JOHN FITZGERALD KENNEDY ❦ ANWAR EL
SADAT ❦ CESAR CHAVEZ ❦ ELIE WIESEL ❦
MARTIN LUTHER KING, JR. ❦ ANNE FRAN
❦ THE DALAI LAMA ❦ WANGARI MAATHA
❦ AUNG SAN SUU KYI ❦ PRINCESS DIANA ❦
RALPH WALDO EMERSON ❦ MAHATM
GANDHI ❦ ALBERT EINSTEIN ❦ ELEANO
ROOSEVELT ❦ RALPH BUNCHE ❦ MOTHE
TERESA ❦ JOHN FITZGERALD KENNEDY

Paths to Peace

People Who Changed the World

Paths to Peace

People Who Changed the World

JANE BRESKIN ZALBEN

DUTTON CHILDREN'S BOOKS

The author would like to thank:

❧ Leo S. Ullman, attorney for the Anne Frank Center USA, 584 Broadway, Suite 408, New York, NY 10012, for sharing all of his and his parents' primary source material from when he was a child hidden in Amsterdam during World War II. Anne Frank photo copyright © AFF/AFH, Basel, Amsterdam.

❧ Jonathan Zalben, for use of a frame from his multimedia performance "Organized Color Intoxication," altered for the Elie Wiesel background, and for creating the graph design for the Albert Einstein piece.

❧ Steven Zalben, for his rainbow photo, altered for the Dalai Lama piece.

❧ AP Photo Archive Internet, for a photo altered for the Cesar Chavez piece.

❧ National Archive Internet, for a photo altered for the Dr. Martin Luther King, Jr. border.

❧ The Port Washington Library reference librarians and Chiara Condi, my research assistant.

DUTTON CHILDREN'S BOOKS
A division of Penguin Young Readers Group

Published by the Penguin Group
Penguin Group (USA) Inc., 375 Hudson Street, New York, New York 10014, U.S.A. • Penguin Group (Canada), 90 Eglinton Avenue East, Suite 700, Toronto, Ontario, Canada M4P 2Y3 (a division of Pearson Penguin Canada Inc.) • Penguin Books Ltd, 80 Strand, London WC2R 0RL, England • Penguin Ireland, 25 St Stephen's Green, Dublin 2, Ireland (a division of Penguin Books Ltd) Penguin Group (Australia), 250 Camberwell Road, Camberwell, Victoria 3124, Australia (a division of Pearson Australia Group Pty Ltd) Penguin Books India Pvt Ltd, 11 Community Centre, Panchsheel Park, New Delhi - 110 017, India • Penguin Group (NZ), Cnr Airborne and Rosedale Roads, Albany, Auckland 1310, New Zealand (a division of Pearson New Zealand Ltd) Penguin Books (South Africa) (Pty) Ltd, 24 Sturdee Avenue, Rosebank, Johannesburg 2196, South Africa Penguin Books Ltd, Registered Offices: 80 Strand, London WC2R 0RL, England

LIBRARY OF CONGRESS CATALOGING-IN-PUBLICATION DATA

Zalben, Jane Breskin.
Paths to peace : people who changed the world / Jane Breskin Zalben.
p. cm.
Includes bibliographical references and index.
ISBN 0-525-47734-9
1. Heroes—Biography—Juvenile literature. 2. Biography—Juvenile literature. I. Title.
CT107.Z35 2006
920'.009'04—dc22   2005013663

Published in the United States by Dutton Children's Books,
a division of Penguin Young Readers Group
345 Hudson Street, New York, New York 10014
www.penguin.com/youngreaders

Designed by Beth Herzog and Gloria Cheng

Manufactured in China
First Edition
1 3 5 7 9 10 8 6 4 2

CONTENTS

For as long as space endures,
And for as long as living beings remain,
Until then may I too abide
To dispel the misery of the world.

Prayer of an eighth-century Buddhist saint
recited by the Dalai Lama each day

AUTHOR'S NOTE

————————

People who become brave leaders often have the vision when they are very young to make the world a better place. The sixteen peacemakers in this book chose vastly different vocations, from politician to scientist to writer to humanitarian to activist. However, many of them can trace their path to peace from childhood—a challenge they overcame, an event that influenced them, or an individual who spurred them on to find the inner strength to do good.

These peacemakers influenced each other as well. Their lives often overlapped as they found shared interests and goals. Ralph Bunche and Eleanor Roosevelt teamed up to promote world peace. Mother Teresa and Princess Diana became friends. Aung San Suu Kyi, Martin Luther King, Jr., Ralph Bunche, Cesar Chevaz, and the Dalai Lama credit their principles to Mahatma Ghandi—his demand for social, political, and ultimately spiritual change without violence inspired their own personal journeys.

These are just a few of the numerous people who make us think about the meaning and purpose of our lives and challenge us to improve the lives of others. The scientist Archimedes (287—212 B.C.), in explaining the principle of the lever, said, "Give me a place to stand, and I will move the world." President John F. Kennedy recast this famous quote in an address to the United Nations: "My fellow inhabitants of this planet: Let us take a stand here in this assembly of nations. And let us see if we, in our own time, can move the world to a just and lasting peace. We can help make the world safe for diversity. For in the final analysis, our most basic common link is that we all inhabit this small planet. We all breathe the same air. We all cherish our children's future. And we are all mortal." A lever is an object that moves another. Our lives are connected, and change can begin with one person. One person *can* make a difference.

Jane Breskin Zalben

"Nothing can bring you peace but yourself."

"Self-Reliance," *Essays: First Series,* March 1841

RALPH WALDO EMERSON

May 25, 1803 *Boston, Massachusetts, born*
April 27, 1882 *Concord, Massachusetts, died*

Imagine a world with no television, movies, or computers, in which there is plenty of time for nature, books, and quiet reflection. That was Ralph Waldo Emerson's world. Emerson is one of America's foremost writers, philosophers, and ministers. Throughout his life he wrote essays on love, friendship, and education; his most famous collection was published in the book *Self-Reliance and Other Essays.* He believed that positive change in the world starts with the individual—by knowing ourselves and trusting our own instincts and feelings, we could begin to transform society. He inspired a spiritual movement called transcendentalism. It appealed to the Puritan heritage of New England and the rugged pioneers heading toward the western frontier during the 1800s.

Determined to put his principles into motion, Emerson took a stand against slavery way before the Civil War and was labeled an early abolitionist. In 1830, the Cherokee Indians were forced off their ancestral land when gold was discovered. Martin Van Buren became president in 1837 and continued to enforce these policies. Emerson sent a letter of protest to a newspaper publicly reprimanding the president, and when it went unnoticed, he told a friend it "blackened my days and nights." Native Americans were relocated all the way from Georgia to Oklahoma in a march that took place between 1838 and 1839, called the Trail of Tears.

In a speech entitled "War" that Emerson gave to the American Peace Society in 1838, he compared war to his favorite theme, nature: "The microscope reveals small biters that swim and fight in an illuminated drop of water; and the little globe is but a too faithful miniature of the large." These words are as relevant now as they were three centuries ago. Ralph Waldo Emerson's thinking was way ahead of his time, and his philosophy resonates today.

"We must be the change we wish to see in the world."

Indian Opinion, Gandhi's newspaper in South Africa, September 8, 1913

MAHATMA GANDHI

October 2, 1869 *Porbandar, India, born*
January 30, 1948 *New Delhi, India, assassinated*

Mohandas Karamchand Gandhi grew up in India. As a young British-trained lawyer on his way to South Africa in 1893, he had a first-class train ticket but was told to sit in the baggage car when a white passenger objected. Over this defining moment in his life when his rights were denied, he sued the railroad, won, and became a leader of nonwhites, organizing the first nonviolent mass-movement protest.

Gandhi returned to India in 1915, determined to free his country of centuries of British rule and to topple its caste system, which separated society into different classes according to birth. He believed that injuring one's enemy can cause one to become likc that enemy; therefore, he wanted to bring about change without violence. Through organized strikes, fasts, and protests—which Gandhi termed acts of "noncooperation," "civil disobedience," and "passive resistance"—he brought world attention to his situation. He encouraged millions to boycott British-made cloth and spin their own instead. His plain, loose-fitting garment became a symbol of his Hindu heritage and independence. During the Amritsar Massacre in 1919 at a holy Sikh shrine, the British opened fire on an unarmed crowd that was celebrating a festival, killing around four hundred people. Gandhi fasted to show his opposition and told his followers not to hurt anyone. In 1930, he led the famous Salt March, protesting the India Salt Act of 1882, which taxed salt, a necessity, and forced Indians to buy from the British. On a two-hundred-mile walk to the ocean, Gandhi gathered sea salt along beaches and was joined by thousands of supporters in an effort to prove that salt belonged to everyone. In 1947, Gandhi finally won independence for India from British control, and he did so without weapons. He led his country to freedom, paving the way for future leaders who adopted his nonviolent means. The lives Gandhi inspired stretch across the globe.

"Out of clutter, find simplicity.
From discord, find harmony.
In the middle of difficulty lies opportunity."

Einstein's *Three Rules of Work*

ALBERT EINSTEIN

March 14, 1879 *Ulm, Germany, born*
April 18, 1955 *Princeton, New Jersey, died*

A lbert Einstein, considered to be the genius of modern science in the twentieth century, challenged the way we think about the universe in spite of his having had a difficult childhood. Einstein was so shy, he didn't learn to speak until he was three years old, and many considered him to be simple. He failed an exam that would have allowed him to get a diploma as an electrical engineer—his father's trade—so instead he studied mathematics and physics in Zürich, hoping to become a university teacher. After graduation, when he couldn't find a teaching job, his father helped him get a position in the patent office in Switzerland. During his downtime, he scribbled mathematical equations and left them in a desk drawer. From these notes, Einstein developed the Quantum Theory of Light, which won him the Nobel Prize for Physics in 1921 on the photoelectric effect.

Most people think of Einstein as a mathematician and don't realize he was also a peacemaker. World War I brought out his pacifist sympathies—he was no longer shy about speaking out. He signed many peace petitions and antiwar manifestos. In 1929, he appealed to British Palestine to end death sentences for Arab rioters. When the Hitler regime threatened the safety of Jews in Germany, Einstein immigrated to the United States to teach at Princeton University. The Nazis burned all the papers he had left behind. He temporarily abandoned his pacifism in 1939 and sent a letter to President Franklin D. Roosevelt, warning him to take action against Hitler's aggression. In 1944, he handwrote his entire paper on relativity—which dealt with gravity, motion, the speed of light, time and space—to be auctioned for the war effort. It raised six million dollars. Given Einstein's belief in world peace, it is ironic that his work led to the creation of the atomic bomb. One week before his death, he urged all nations to give up nuclear weapons and argued for international peace.

"If we want a free and peaceful world, if we want the deserts to bloom, and man to grow to greater dignity as a human being — WE CAN DO IT!"

Tomorrow Is Now, published in November 1963

ELEANOR ROOSEVELT

October 11, 1884 *New York, New York, born*
November 7, 1962 *New York, New York, died*

———————

Eleanor Roosevelt always thought of herself as an "ugly duckling," yet she spent her life in the public eye, giving a voice to the oppressed. She attended a boarding school as a teenager and blossomed under the guidance of a teacher who exposed the students to a world wider than one of privilege.

Politics was in her family's blood. Her uncle Theodore Roosevelt became president of the United States in 1901, and in 1905, Eleanor married her distant cousin, Franklin Delano Roosevelt, who became a New York state senator in 1911. Eleanor's own political interests flourished. She became active in the Red Cross, volunteering in hospitals. The summer of 1921 was a turning point in her life, when her husband contracted polio. Eleanor urged him to continue his career, telling him, "You must do the thing you think you cannot do." An equal partner, she went where he couldn't, to deliver speeches, offer advice, and help him campaign. From 1933 to 1945, during her husband's presidency throughout the Great Depression and World War II, she gave hope to refugees and to the hungry, homeless, and jobless. This mother of five fought to pass laws concerning the rights of women and children. In 1939, when the Daughters of the American Revolution wouldn't allow Marian Anderson to perform in Constitution Hall because she was black, Eleanor invited Anderson to sing on the steps of the Lincoln Memorial instead.

Eleanor Roosevelt changed the role of First Lady forever. She held press conferences, wrote a newspaper column every day, and had a radio show in which she expressed opinions on social causes such as racism, bigotry, poverty, child labor, and world peace. She traveled the globe, raising money for UNICEF on behalf of children in need, and became a delegate three times and Chair to the United Nations Commission on Human Rights. Mrs. Roosevelt was "First Lady of the World."

13

"I have a bias against war;
a bias for peace.
I have a bias that leads me to
believe in the essential goodness of
my fellow man ...
that no problem of human relations
is ever insoluble."

Speech to the American Association
for the United Nations, 1949

RALPH BUNCHE

August 7, 1904 *Detroit, Michigan, born*
December 9, 1971 *New York, New York, died*

During the civil rights movement of the mid-1960s, Dr. Bunche said, "I am a Negro, I am also an American. This is my country. I own a share in it. . . . My ancestors helped create it, to build it, to make it strong and great, and rich. All of this belongs to me as much as it belongs to any American with a white skin." And yet, Ralph Johnson Bunche's journey wasn't an easy one. There were many bumps in the road. But thanks to the loving support of his grandmother, "Nana," they didn't hold him back. Both parents had died by the time he was eleven. When he and Nana moved to an all-white neighborhood, the landlord tried to prevent them from going into their home. He wasn't permitted to swim in a pool with friends because a sign read, NO COLORED ALLOWED. His name was left off the honor roll in his high school, even though he graduated number one in his class.

Against all odds, Ralph Bunche became a man of many "firsts." He was the first African-American to get a graduate degree in political science from Harvard. He was a founding member of the United Nations. In 1950, he was the first person of African ancestry to receive the Nobel Peace Prize, for helping to negotiate a treaty during the 1948 Arab-Israeli War. And, in 1949, the National Association for the Advancement of Colored People (NAACP) awarded him the Spingarn Medal, its highest honor. After World War II, because of their shared interests, he teamed up with Eleanor Roosevelt to promote world peace by forming human rights treaties during sessions of the General Assembly in the United Nations. During international peacekeeping missions, he insisted that all UN observers remain unarmed. On his death, it was said that "He belonged to every nation on earth that yearns for peace."

"Good works are a link forming a chain of love around the world."

On the opening of the Missionaries of Charity, Calcutta, October 7, 1950

MOTHER TERESA

August 27, 1910 *Skopje, Yugoslavia (now Macedonia), born*
September 5, 1997 *Calcutta, India, died*

Agnes Gonxha Bojaxhiu was a teacher and a nun before she took the name Mother Teresa and became a missionary for needy people throughout the world. At the age of twelve, she felt called by God to help people. Six years later, she left her home in Yugoslavia and joined an order of nuns in Ireland to learn English and train as an educator. From there she followed her dream of teaching in India and went to St. Mary's convent in Calcutta. At twenty-one, she took her first religious vows, receiving the name Sister Teresa. In 1946, she got her "second calling"—to devote herself completely to helping those less fortunate by living among them. Called the "saint of the gutter," she lived in the slums of Calcutta, founded shelters for countless orphans, and traveled the world, aiding and creating clinics. The Pope allowed Sister Teresa to set up a new order of nuns outside of St. Mary's, and in 1950, she established the Missionaries of Charity and became known as Mother Teresa.

Although she had been nominated for the Nobel Peace Prize twice before, for her work on behalf of the homeless, it wasn't until 1979 that Mother Teresa became the sixth woman to receive it. Dressed in her usual simple sari with white-and-blue-striped borders, she accepted the award in support of the people she helped—the sick and impoverished. She told the audience they "had been created to live God's gift of peace." She used the cash award to open homes for lepers and build more centers for the poor and dying.

Mother Teresa became an honorary citizen of the United States in 1996 and was given the Congressional Gold Medal of Honor the following year. Her selflessness as a humanitarian touched millions, and is encapsulated in her words: "If we have no peace, it is because we have forgotten that we belong to each other."

"The earth, the sea, and the air are the concern of every nation."

An address before the Eighteenth General Assembly of the United Nations, September 20, 1963

JOHN FITZGERALD KENNEDY

May 29, 1917 *Brookline, Massachusetts, born*
November 22, 1963 *Dallas, Texas, assassinated*

The first-born son in the Kennedy family, Joe Jr., was raised to become president from the day he was born. When he died tragically, his father chose Joe Jr.'s younger brother, John, to fulfill this dream. Joe Jr. was a tough act to follow. John Fitzgerald Kennedy, who suffered from Addison's disease and was ill throughout his life, overcame pain every step of the way. He joined the navy during World War II, saved the crew of his patrol boat, PT-109, and received a medal for courage. After the war, he secured a seat in the Eleventh Congressional District of Massachusetts. Once in the Senate, in 1953, he became the first member from New England to appoint an African-American to his staff. He wrote a book about eight courageous politicians called *Profiles in Courage,* which won the Pulitzer Prize. All of this set the stage for his running for president of the United States. He became the first Catholic president in 1961, making his father proud.

In his inaugural address, President Kennedy said, "Ask not what your country can do for you—ask what you can do for your country." Among his many lasting accomplishments is the Peace Corps, a government agency that sends thousands of young volunteers to underdeveloped countries to promote world peace. He avoided a nuclear confrontation with the Soviet Union during the Cuban Missile Crisis in 1962, and a year later both nations signed a Nuclear Test Ban Treaty, creating a "hot line" so leaders could talk instantly in a crisis. In his Food for Peace program, he sold wheat to Russia with the hope that every hungry child would receive nourishment. He took a stand against racism, welcoming Martin Luther King, Jr. and other civil rights leaders to the White House. Kennedy believed that "Peace is a daily, a weekly, a monthly process, gradually changing opinions, slowly eroding old barriers, quietly building new structures."

19

"Peace is much more precious than a piece of land."

Speech in Cairo, March 8, 1978

Peace

salam   سلام

shalom   שלום

ANWAR EL-SADAT

December 25, 1918 *Mit Abu al-Kum, Egypt, born*
October 6, 1981 *Cairo, Egypt, assassinated*

As a child, Anwar Sadat saw his country suffer under British occupation and dreamed of an independent Egypt. His parents, devout Muslims with little money, struggled to send him to religious schools to study the Koran. His father, a clerk in an army hospital, helped him get into the Royal Military Academy, from which he graduated in 1938. Sadat became an officer with a role in the government. Like Gandhi, Sadat sought freedom for his country, but unlike Gandhi, he didn't use peaceful means. During World War II, he formed a revolutionary group that sided with the Germans to weaken England's control of Egypt. After the war, he was jailed and dismissed as an officer, but, years later, he was reinstated in the army with the help of high-level friends. Sadat, Gamal Abdel Nasser, and the Free Officers Organization planned a revolution to overthrow the British. In 1956, Egypt got its first president: Nasser, and he appointed Sadat as vice president. Sadat's dream had come true. Under President Nasser, Sadat rose to power, eventually becoming president when Nasser died in 1970.

As president, Sadat wanted peace between Egypt and Israel. He offered to come to Jerusalem in 1977 when no Arab leader had done that before. This lone, brave step stirred strong resentment from surrounding Arab nations. His initiative led to the Camp David Accords: in 1978 U.S. president Jimmy Carter invited President Sadat and the Israeli prime minister, Menachem Begin, to Camp David, a presidential retreat, to negotiate a peace treaty. Signed at the White House, the agreement marked the first time a Middle Eastern state recognized Israel as a country. During that same year, Begin and Sadat were cowinners of the Nobel Peace Prize for trying to make peace in an area "shadowed by war." In his book *In Search of Identity* Sadat repeated his grandmother's words: "Land is immortal, for it harbors the mysteries of creation. A man's village is his peace of mind."

21

"Non–violence in action is a very potent force . . .
If we have the patience, things will change."

Newspaper interview, "Apostle of Non-Violence," *Observer,* May 1970

CESAR CHAVEZ

March 31, 1927 *near Yuma, Arizona, born*
April 23, 1993 *San Luis, Arizona, died*

For someone who was poor most of his life, Cesar Chavez was "rich" in an essential way. He was raised in a loving Mexican-American family. As migrant farm workers, they picked crops for landowners all day, but they could barely afford to buy food for themselves. He saw children do backbreaking work and laborers exposed to pesticides in sun-blistering fields. Chavez began to realize what many minority people had learned: he had to organize, educate, and empower his people. He saw Mahatma Gandhi free a whole nation through nonviolence and believed he could do the same. As a farm worker in California, he joined the local Community Service Organization, a prominent Latino civil rights group. Then, in 1962, he founded the National Farm Workers Association, which later became the United Farm Workers of America. The first successful farm workers' union in U.S. history, it organized laborers under the banner of *La Causa* (Spanish for "The Cause") so they could have health benefits, wage increases, and better working conditions. *"Huelga!"*—"Strike!"—became the workers' cry. They would stop work in the fields and initiate protests with marches, picketing, and prayer. Chavez himself fasted. He asked people not to buy lettuce and grapes (the crops the workers grew) in the supermarket. This grape boycott, as it was known, was one of the longest in history, lasting five years. Chavez was driven by one goal: to see all Hispanic farm workers treated as important human beings. His efforts resulted in new labor laws that improved conditions for the people who grew food in our nation.

In 1994, after Chavez's death, he was honored at the White House as the first Mexican-American to receive the Presidential Medal of Freedom. At the awards ceremony, President Clinton called him "a Moses figure." Cesar Chavez led his people on a remarkable journey through peaceful means.

"Peace is not God's gift to his creatures,
it is our gift to each other."

Nobel Laureate Lecture, Sweden, December 11, 1986

ELIE WIESEL

September 30, 1928 *Sighet, Transylvania (Romania), born*

After accepting the Nobel Peace Prize in 1986, Elie Wiesel stated, "Just as man cannot live without dreams, he cannot live without hope. If dreams reflect the past, hope summons the future." His own dreams had been shattered in the spring of 1944, when he was fifteen. During World War II, he was sent to four concentration death camps simply for being Jewish. After the war, he was taken to an orphanage in France, having survived the trauma of losing both his parents and a younger sister. He took a personal vow not to write about his experiences, but ten years later he decided he could no longer remain silent about how the world had abandoned an entire population of Eastern European Jewry. Wiesel coined the term "the Holocaust" for Nazi Germany's mass slaughter of six million Jews. He became a journalist, a teacher, and a philosopher, in the hope that by sharing his experiences he could prevent such atrocities from ever happening again. In 1958, his first book, *Night,* was published, describing the horrors of his childhood. Now a classic, it has been read by millions in over thirty languages.

As an American citizen and international peacemaker, Wiesel travels to parts of the world where there are hatred, racism, and violence, and is a spokesperson wherever human rights are threatened or violated. Among the many honors he has received are the Presidential Medal of Freedom, the U.S. Congressional Gold Medal, and the French Legion of Honor with the rank of Grand Cross. With the money that accompanied his Nobel Peace Prize, he set up a Foundation for Humanity, with the goal of alerting the world to people's suffering, not allowing it to be ignored as in World War II. If Elie Wiesel's message could be summed up in one word, it would be "Remember."

"Let freedom ring from every hill and molehill . . .
From every mountainside, let freedom ring."

"I Have a Dream" speech, delivered in Washington, D.C., August 28, 1963

MARTIN LUTHER KING, JR.

January 15, 1929 *Atlanta, Georgia, born*
April 4, 1968 *Memphis, Tennessee, assassinated*

Martin Luther King, Jr. grew up in the South during the time of the "Jim Crow laws," when it was illegal for a black person to drink from a "white" water fountain, eat in a "white" restaurant, or go to a school that had been designated for white people only. When Dr. King became a minister, he fought these injustices through nonviolent means. He encouraged African-Americans to eat at "white" lunch counters during sit-ins. He organized "freedom rides," in which black and white people came together to ride segregated buses. In 1955, a woman named Rosa Parks refused to give up her seat to a white man at the bus driver's insistence. When she was arrested, Reverend King asked African-Americans in Montgomery, Alabama, to walk or carpool instead of taking buses for one day. Word spread like wildfire throughout the South. One day extended into many. More and more people did not ride buses. By the time that bus boycott ended—more than a year after it had started—Dr. King and other blacks had won some victories in the fight for integration, but they had also endured death threats and acts of hatred. On January 30, 1956, King calmed an angry crowd as he stood on the bombed-out front porch of his home, saying, "We must meet hate with love."

In the early 1960s, social change wasn't coming fast enough, and riots broke out across the country. Support for King's movement was building, but he needed to stir the hearts of lawmakers. On August 28, 1963, he organized a march on Washington, D.C. On the steps of the Lincoln Memorial, in front of a crowd of about 250,000, he delivered his famous "I Have a Dream" speech. King was awarded the Nobel Peace Prize on December 10, 1964. It would take several more years, more demonstrations, and more personal sacrifices before real change came, but this peaceful pastor inspired countless people to follow in his footsteps.

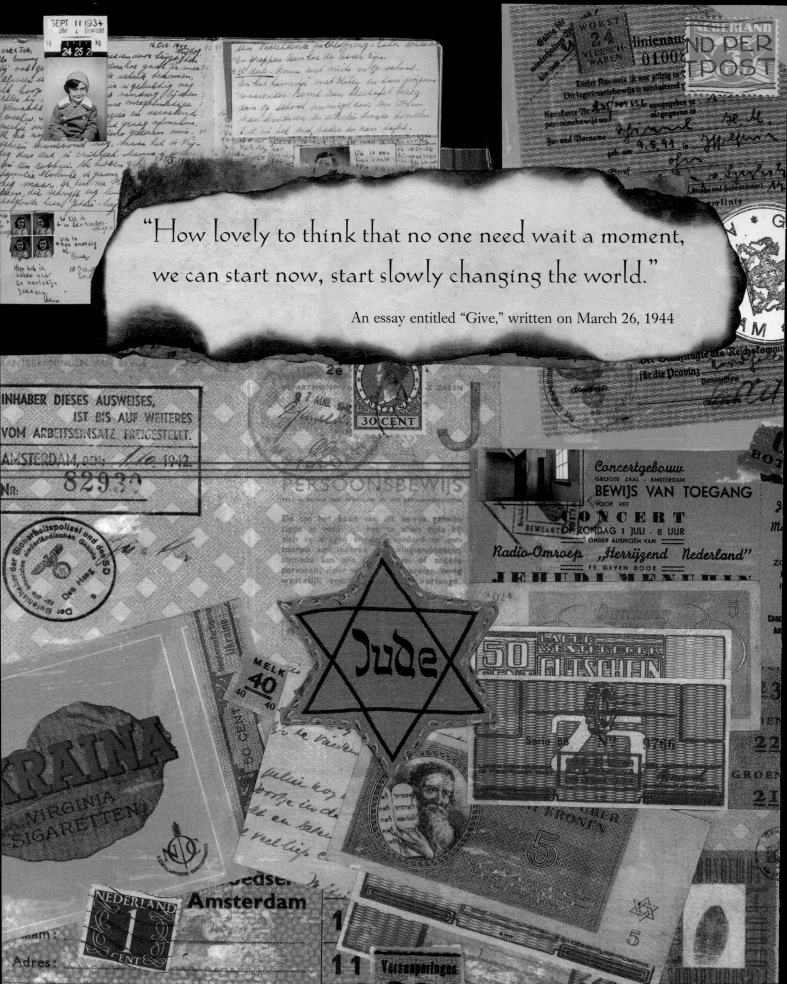

"How lovely to think that no one need wait a moment, we can start now, start slowly changing the world."

An essay entitled "Give," written on March 26, 1944

ANNE FRANK

June 12, 1929 *Frankfurt am Main, Germany, born*
Late February or early March 1945 *Bergen-Belsen concentration camp, Germany, died*

———————————

Anne Frank dreamed of becoming a writer or a movie star. But in 1934, Germany was not a safe place for a Jewish child. Adolf Hitler, the chancellor, began a campaign against Jewish citizens. So Anne's father, Otto, moved the family to Amsterdam, where he thought life would be better. At first it was. Then, in 1940, Hitler invaded the Netherlands. Jews were forced to sew yellow stars on their clothing. They were not allowed to work, attend school, or go to public places. For a young girl like Anne, these restrictions made life unbearable.

On July 6, 1942, after the family was notified that Anne's sixteen-year-old sister would be deported to a Nazi labor camp, the Franks decided to go into hiding. Along with four other people, they moved into a secret annex—hidden rooms— above the building where Otto Frank had his spice business. Anne took along a diary her parents had given her a month earlier, on her thirteenth birthday. In the pages of this red-and-white-checked album fastened with a brass lock, the heart of an extraordinary girl living in an unimaginable time was unlocked. Anne composed short stories, fairy tales, essays, and letters that revealed her innermost thoughts, ideas, and emotions to an unknown audience. Little did she know that her diary would become world-famous. Two years later, the Franks' hiding place was discovered, and the family was taken to Auschwitz, a concentration camp in Poland. Anne and her sister were sent a month later to another camp, Bergen-Belsen, where both of them died. Miep Gies, a family friend, found the diary after Anne's death. Otto Frank, the only family member who survived the Holocaust, decided to share her story with the world. Published in 1947, *The Diary of Anne Frank* gave voice to millions of other victims and at the same time encouraged readers to believe in humankind in the face of tragedy. As Anne wrote in her diary, ". . . in spite of everything, I still believe that people are really good at heart."

29

"Inner peace is the true foundation of world peace."

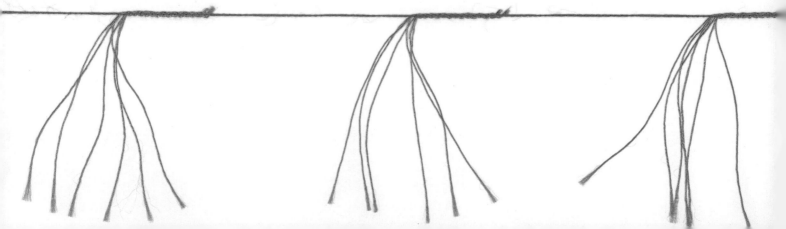

Message to the United Nations Millennium World Peace Summit, August 23, 2000

THE DALAI LAMA

July 6, 1935 *Taktser, Tibet, born*

High up in the mountains of Tibet, an ordinary boy, Lhamo Thondup, was born to peasant farmers. At age two, his parents believed he was the reincarnation of the Thirteenth Dalai Lama, leader of Tibet. Their belief was confirmed by other spiritual leaders. From the time he was four years old, he was raised as His Holiness, the Fourteenth Dalai Lama, and taught by Buddhist monks to become Tibet's future leader. (*Dalai* means "ocean" in Mongolian and *lama* is "teacher" in Tibetan. The two words combined mean "ocean of wisdom.") When he was twenty-four years old, this revered man was forced to flee his country because of the violent Chinese occupation in 1959. For over forty years, he has lived in exile in the Himalayan town of Dharamsala, India, but he remains the spiritual and political leader of Tibet. His goal is to return to his homeland someday by making peace with China through nonviolent means.

The Dalai Lama feels a responsibility to deliver a message of peace and interfaith tolerance to the world: We are all part of one large family. In 1967, he made his first trip outside of India to get international support to free his country, make people aware of human rights violations against his people, and keep Tibetan culture alive. Since then, he has tirelessly continued to meet world leaders in this effort, and through his travels he has helped thousands of refugees in India, Europe, and other parts of the globe. His kindness and compassion were recognized in 1989, when he was awarded the Nobel Peace Prize, which he accepted on behalf of the Tibetan people. In his Nobel Lecture he said, "Maybe we have different clothes, our skin is of a different color, or we speak different languages. That is on the surface. But basically, we are the same human beings. . . . Because we all share this small planet earth, we have to learn to live in harmony and peace with each other and with nature. That is not just a dream, but a necessity."

"In managing our resources . . . we plant the seeds of peace."

Norwegian TV2 interview reported in *The New York Times*, October 9, 2004

WANGARI MAATHAI

April 1, 1940 *Nyeri, Kenya, Africa, born*

———————

Wangari Maathai, a member of the Kikuyu tribe, was raised on a farm in Kenya. Her parents felt she should attend school instead of fulfilling the traditional role of women in the village: doing household chores. And so the eldest daughter of six children became a pioneer. She received her college degree in the United States on a Kennedy scholarship and was the first woman in East and Central Africa to earn a Ph.D. Dr. Maathai became director of the Kenya Red Cross. She was the first female chair of the Veterinary Anatomy Department at the University of Nairobi. She ran unsuccessfully for the presidency of Kenya, but years later was elected to the parliament. At this time, she is assistant minister of Environment, Natural Resources and Wildlife. None of this came without a struggle. Maathai has been imprisoned many times for protesting the clearing of Kenyan forests. She dissented by planting trees on farms, in schoolyards, and on church grounds. Since 1977, she has organized poor women to plant over thirty million trees. It began with a handful of seedlings in her backyard and grew to her paying women for every tree that took root. In 1993, she received the Jane Addams International Women's Leadership Award, for standing up to a society that discriminated against women and ignored conservation in third-world countries.

In 2004, Dr. Maathai became the first African woman to be awarded the Nobel Peace Prize, for founding the Green Belt Movement in East Africa. Many people wondered, *What does planting trees have to do with peace?* But forests are essential for preventing soil erosion and providing shade, fuel, building material, and food. By teaching people to care for themselves and the environment, she has helped them meet their basic needs. Dr. Maathai feels that "when you destroy the environment, you will have conflict." One woman's strength has given Kenya's children a future. Maathai remains sturdy and unbending, like the trees she plants.

"Everyone should be given a chance to create
peace and harmony in their own way."

An interview during PeaceJam, published in the *Shambala Sun,* January 1996

AUNG SAN SUU KYI

June 19, 1945 *Rangoon, Burma (now Yangon, Myanmar), born*

Aung San Suu Kyi is the daughter of Burma's national hero, General Aung San, who was assassinated when she was two years old. This once-privileged daughter has dedicated her life to fighting for Burma's independence from a military dictatorship. In 1988, her fellow citizens revolted against the repressive "junta" regime that had ruled for twenty-six years. Suu Kyi became the leader of this movement for change, helping to found the National League for Democracy, whose aim was to restore democratic government in the country. Considering her a threat, the existing rulers of Burma placed her under "house arrest" and refused to hand over power to the new government, even when the NLD won a 1990 election by a landslide. Despite being imprisoned in her home and isolated from her family, she continued her efforts to free her country and went on a hunger strike. As a human rights activist, she was awarded the Nobel Peace Prize in 1991 for working to achieve freedom for Myanmar through peaceful means while she was held in captivity. Not allowed to receive this honor in person, she sent her two teenage sons to Oslo to accept it on her behalf. Seven previous Nobel laureates flew to see Suu Kyi in her country, but they were denied entry. They called for her release and offered their support. In 1999, her government prevented her from traveling to London to say good-bye to her dying husband, whom she had not seen for four years.

On May 6, 2002, Suu Kyi was finally released from house arrest, but she did not stop pursuing her goal of democracy. In a seemingly endless cycle, this determined woman continues to fight for independence and continues to be jailed and abused. She is now the world's most famous political prisoner. All this mother wants is peace; and she is willing to fight for it with patience, resolve, and courage.

"Everyone needs to be valued. Everyone has the potential to give something back if they only had the chance."

Acceptance speech for the Humanitarian of the Year Award, New York, December 1995

PRINCESS DIANA

July 1, 1961 *Norfolk, England, born*
August 31, 1997 *Paris, France, died*

Diana Frances Spencer had compassion for the common man even though she was part of the royal family. In an interview with the BBC, she said that the "biggest disease this world suffers from in this day and age is the disease of people feeling unloved." Her mother left her marriage when Diana was very young. At the age of nine a devastated Diana went away to school, taking her favorite pet guinea pig, Peanuts. She tried to cure her loneliness by taking care of many animals in her free time. Perhaps it isn't surprising, then, that she grew up to become a loving kindergarten teacher who wanted to make things right for children from the very start. But on July 29, 1981, she left that life behind, and became the Princess of Wales, when she married Prince Charles, the future king of England. This twenty year-old, known as "Shy Di," was not too shy to take on many different causes: working for the Red Cross during disasters and helping AIDS patients, battered women, the homeless, and people with leprosy. Many in her position would have ignored public work, but Princess Di tirelessly sought out those who suffered. In January 1997 she visited Angola, and after spending time with victims of land mines, she set out to have those explosives banned globally. She brought her message to Bosnia, and in June visited First Lady Hillary Clinton in the United States to make the world aware that land mines maim and kill thousands of children each year. In New York City that same summer, she met Mother Teresa, who became a friend and mentor. Mother Teresa said, "Everywhere there is a need for giving, and Diana has more influence over the British people than anybody else."

After dying in a tragic car accident, Diana left behind millions of mourners as well as an enduring legacy of compassion. This humane woman, referred to as an "English Rose," accomplished a lot in her brief life to make the world a better place.

ART NOTES

Since I was a teenager, I have been collecting papers and fabrics from around the world; many are included in the illustrations. The stamps in the border art throughout are original—many, in mint condition. (I was an avid collector as a child.)

TITLE PAGE – Each person creates peace in their own way. For me, it was through knitting—an activity I had never done until recently, when I was recuperating from an illness. It was meditative, and I became passionate about knitting, so I added a swatch to the art.

EMERSON – I wanted to portray an "illuminated drop of water" in nature, like Thoreau's Walden Pond, which I visited during the making of this book, since Emerson influenced Thoreau. This famous pond is surprisingly small. The facing-page border art is composed of dried leaves.

GANDHI – I used real sea-salt crystals from the beach and Indian paper for the border.

EINSTEIN – The background is patterned with his equations. An acetate overlay indicates abstract clutter versus the simple shape of the sixties peace symbol sculpted in metal: discord and harmony.

ROOSEVELT – I painted an etching that I made a long time ago. The border represents the "blooming" of her passions.

BUNCHE – His life was spent trying to heal Israeli-Arab relations through the United Nations. He personally suffered and overcame much prejudice. A black and a white dove express his plight.

MOTHER TERESA – Blue stripes are painted on linen canvas to replicate the sari she always wore.

KENNEDY – This is a collage of the earth, sea, and air using varied materials: cotton, string, paper, and sandpaper. My husband and I decided to renovate our house while I was doing this book. When we opened the walls, I found the article on "Jack" (Kennedy's nickname) crumpled between the studs.

EL-SADAT – The calligraphy is on white opaline parchment and the surrounding matte is antique parchment. The border is paper made from papyrus from the Nile River. The old money is real. Both the paper and the money were brought back from Cairo, Egypt, when I visited schoolchildren in the Cairo American College in 1995.

CHAVEZ – The watercolor/collage is of parents and children picking farm crops under the sun. This is juxtaposed with the border showing labels that I collected from fruit in the market and a tiny photo of Chavez picketing. The eagle symbol is that of the United Farm Workers Association.

WIESEL – This is hand-painted coarse sandpaper; wire twisted to look like barbed wire; flowers I grew, pressed, and painted; and a digitally rendered video frame behind art of nighttime.

KING – The art is photography and cut-paper collage, evoking the Ebenezer Baptist Church where King preached and the hills and valleys I saw when I went to Africa to speak in schools. Within the border is an article about a boycott in Birmingham from the 1962 *New York Herald Tribune*—a piece of newspaper I serendipitously found inside the walls of my house. There are also an altered photo of one of his marches, part of a quote from *The Wall Street Journal,* hand-painted-art, and graffiti in oil crayon.

FRANK – Leo Ullman was a hidden child in Amsterdam, Holland. The materials in the collage were saved by his family. The star is a version of what was worn on clothing, reduced by half. Within the art are "Jewish" money, an identity card with the letter *J* on it, a transit pass, food stamps, a concert ticket from when life was "normal," a thumbprint for identity, and Russian cigarettes used as barter for food. I also included portions of postcards showing photographs of Anne's diary and of her as a child. The two stamps are from my childhood collection, and they are exactly the same as the ones that were in Anne's diary. The border, created on the computer, replicates the fabric that covered her diary.

DALAI LAMA – The main image is a digitally altered photo taken in Vermont. The rainbow and the mountains evoke the high Himalayas. The spot ornaments are watercolors of a design found on Tibetan nuns' drums (p. 4), and the lotus symbol represents the Buddhist belief that the potential for good is in all of us. In the border art, the colors of maroon and saffron are worn by Tibetan monks. The fabrics are Asian. The gold incense paper is burned when prayers are recited. The gold flecks remind me of the monks' endless, laborious hours creating art out of grains of sand in mandalas (a mandala is a Hindu or Buddhist graphic symbol of the universe), only to erase it in one quick gesture to show that life is fleeting.

MAATHAI – The collage has shredded wheat, burlap, bancha-tea twigs, and bark from African trees. I also used acrylic gel and gesso on autumn leaves to show the connections between the environment, people planting, and peace.

SUU KYI – I saw a photo of her in the jungle garden where she stays secluded and writes. I wanted to wrap her in a quilt of tranquillity, so I sewed a small one. Raffia rope and a vine that I grew in my backyard were pressed and intertwined with textiles. The cloth is from Thailand, Laos, Cambodia, and surrounding Southeast Asia, which I incorporated with pale-green-grass rice paper, to suggest Suu Kyi under house arrest.

PRINCESS DIANA – Diana is often referred to as an "English Rose." I created a watercolor of a child to symbolize how she touched children of all nations. One of the stamps is of her son, Prince William.

GLOSSARY

abolitionist: a person who believed that slavery was wrong and should be abolished.

Addison's disease: characterized by weakness and low blood pressure, due to decreased secretion of cortisol.

boycott: an organized refusal to buy a product or use a service, as a nonviolent means of bringing about social and political change.

Camp David: a retreat in Maryland where the U.S. president rests or hosts special guests. Often important meetings of world leaders take place in its conference facility.

caste system: ranks a hereditary social group by class, according to education, occupation, economic standing, and/or religion. The position of the individual within the class limits or gives privileges. In India, in Hindu society, one is born into a low or high caste.

chancellor: the chief minister of a state in certain parliamentary governments.

civil rights movement: organized action during the 1960s to defend and extend rights of full social, legal, and economic equality to African-Americans.

concentration camp: a guarded compound for members of an ethnic race or minority group or political prisoners, particularly those established by the Nazis in Germany during World War II to persecute and kill Jews, homosexuals, Gypsies, and opponents of the regime.

Congressional Gold Medal of Honor: the highest award that the U.S. Congress can bestow.

democracy: government by the people, in which leaders are elected in a voting system available to all citizens.

Holocaust: the mass slaughter of European Jews and others in concentration camps during World War II.

humanitarian: promoting social reform, having concern for or helping other people to improve.

integration: to bring together as equals different racial, religious, or ethnic groups.

Jim Crow laws: state laws in the southern United States that enforced segregation and legalized discrimination against black people in public places, on public transportation, etc.

junta: a small group ruling a country after seizing power by force.

Koran: the sacred text of Islam, written by the prophet Mohammed; the foundation of Muslim law, dictating religion, culture, and politics.

labor movement: an organized effort to support and change the conditions of workers through unions.

lepers: a group of people ostracized and rejected because of the disfiguring skin disease of leprosy.

manifesto: a public opinion or declaration of intention issued by a group.

migrant worker: a farm laborer who looks for work in different areas and harvests crops seasonally.

missionary: a person sent by a church into an area of poverty to promote religion, to educate, and to do hospital work.

Nobel Peace Prize: Alfred B. Nobel, the Swedish inventor of dynamite, established in his will an annual monetary prize for an individual's outstanding achievement in promoting peace. The award was first given in 1901.

nuclear: pertaining to or involving atomic weapons, or operated by atomic energy.

occupation: the control and possession of land by foreign military forces.

pacifist: someone who believes in peace, opposes war or violence, and refuses to serve in the military.

PeaceJam: international education program built around Nobel Peace laureates who personally work with youth to pass on the spirit, skills, and wisdom they embody.

petition: a formal request to a power of authority that bears a list of supporters' names.

polio: inflammation of the spinal cord resulting in paralysis.

Presidential Medal of Freedom: an honor awarded by the president of the United States to any citizen who makes an exceptional contribution to the nation and/or a significant endeavor toward world peace.

Pulitzer Prize: an annual award established by the journalist Joseph Pulitzer, first given in 1917, to honor the finest achievement in literature, journalism, photography, or music.

Quantum Theory of Light: Einstein received the Nobel Prize in Physics in 1921 for discovering this phenomenon of the photoelectric effect. He found that when you shine a light upon certain metals, a stream of particles (called photons/electrons) is emitted.

regime: a system of rule or a government in power.

reincarnation: the belief that after death, the soul is reborn and returns to earth in another body or form.

relativity: a complex physics theory, developed by Albert Einstein, that all motion can be defined in terms of space, time, and gravity: $E=mc^2$. (E is energy; m is mass; c is the speed of light squared.) This equation affected the ideas of space travel, gravity, electromagnetism, and the development of the atom bomb.

revolutionary: a sudden, complete, or marked change outside the usual procedure or principles; a person or idea that is radically new and different from the establishment.

sari: a long, wrapped garment worn by Hindu women.

segregation: separation of racial, ethnic, and religious groups.

Sikh: a religion in India that refuses to recognize the Hindu caste system.

Spingarn Medal: annual award established by Joel Elias Spingarn, Chairman of the National Association for the Advancement of Colored People (NAACP), in 1914 to be given to a black American for outstanding achievement.

transcendentalism: a philosophy associated with Ralph Waldo Emerson, among others, that emphasizes spiritual thought over practical experience.

treaty: a formal agreement between two or more states or countries—to bring about peace, for example, or to regulate trade.

UNICEF: the United Nations International Children's Emergency Fund, which improves health and nutrition in the world.

union: an alliance or a state of being united.

United Nations: an international organization formed in 1945 to promote peace, security, and cooperation among the countries of the world.

BIBLIOGRAPHY

RALPH WALDO EMERSON

Allen, Gay Wilson. *Waldo Emerson: A Biography.* New York: Viking, 1981.

Derleth, August. *Emerson, Our Contemporary.* New York: Crowell-Collier/Macmillan, 1970.

Emerson, Ralph Waldo. "Self-Reliance." *Essays.* Boston: Self-published sermons, primary source, March 1841.

McAleer, John. *Ralph Waldo Emerson: Days of Encounter.* Boston: Little, Brown, 1984.

Mills, Josephine. *Ralph Waldo Emerson.* Minneapolis: University of Minnesota Press, 1964.

MAHATMA GANDHI

Dalton, Dennis. *Mahatma Gandhi: Nonviolent Power in Action.* New York: Columbia University Press, 1993.

Reeve, Susan. *Choose Peace and Happiness.* Boston: Red Wheel, 2003.

Severance, John B. *Gandhi, Great Soul.* New York: Clarion, 1997.

ALBERT EINSTEIN

Calaprice, Alice, ed. *The Quotable Einstein.* Princeton, NJ: Princeton University Press, 1996.

Lepscky, Ibi. *Albert Einstein.* New York: Barron's, 1982.

MacLeod, Elizabeth. *Albert Einstein: A Life of a Genius.* Toronto: Kids Can Press, 2003.

Nathan, Otto, and Heinz Norden. *Einstein on Peace.* New York: Simon & Schuster, 1960.

ELEANOR ROOSEVELT

Freeman, Russell. *Eleanor Roosevelt: A Life of Discovery.* New York: Clarion, 1993.

Roosevelt, Eleanor. *Tomorrow Is Now.* New York: Harper & Row, 1963.

Weidt, Maryann N. *Stateswoman to the World: A Story About Eleanor Roosevelt.* Minneapolis: Carolrhoda, 1991.

RALPH BUNCHE

Cornell, Jean Gay. *Ralph Bunche: Champion of Peace.* Champaign, IL: Garrard Publishing Co., 1976.

Henry, Charles P. *Ralph Bunche: Model Negro or American Other?.* New York: New York University Press, 1999.

McKissack, Patricia C., and Fredrick McKissack, Jr. *Ralph J. Bunche: Peacemaker.* Springfield, NJ: Enslow Publishers, 1991.

Schraff, Anne. *Ralph Bunche: Winner of the Nobel Peace Prize.* Springfield, NJ: Enslow Publishers, 1999.

Urquhart, Brian. *Ralph Bunche: An American Life.* New York: W. W. Norton, 1993.

MOTHER TERESA

Giff, Patricia Reilly. *Mother Teresa: Sister to the Poor.* New York: Viking Penguin, 1998.

Morgan, Nina. *Mother Teresa: Saint of the Poor.* Austin, TX: Raintree Steck-Vaughn Co., 1998.

Rice, Tanya. *The Life and Times of Mother Teresa.* Philadelphia: Chelsea House, 1998.

JOHN FITZGERALD KENNEDY

Dallek, Robert. *An Unfinished Life: John F. Kennedy.* Boston: Little, Brown, 2003.

Kennedy, John F. *A Strategy of Peace.* Commencement Address. American University, Washington, D.C., 1963.

Usham, Michael V. *The Importance of John F. Kennedy.* San Diego: Lucent Books, 1999.

ANWAR EL-SADAT

Rosen, Deborah Nodler. *Anwar el-Sadat: Middle East Peacemaker*. Chicago: Childrens Press, 1986.

CESAR CHAVEZ

Griswold del Castillo, Richard, and Richard A. Garcia. *César Chávez: A Triumph of Spirit*. Norman, OK: University of Oklahoma Press, 1995.

Roberts, Naurice. *Cesar Chavez and La Causa*. Chicago: Childrens Press, 1986.

ELIE WIESEL

Rittner, Carol, ed. *Elie Wiesel: Between Memory and Hope*. New York: New York University Press, 1990.

Wiesel, Elie. *All Rivers Run to the Sea: Memoirs*. New York: Knopf, 1995.

MARTIN LUTHER KING, JR.

Bull, Angela. *Free at Last: The Story of Martin Luther King, Jr.* New York: Dorling Kindersley, 2000.

Haskins, Jim. *I Have a Dream: The Life and Words of Martin Luther King, Jr.* Brookfield, CT: Millbrook Press, 1992.

King, Martin Luther, Jr. *Stride Toward Freedom: The Montgomery Story*. New York: Harper & Row, 1958.

ANNE FRANK

Bull, Angela. *Anne Frank*. London: Hamish Hamilton, 1984.

Hurwitz, Johanna. *Anne Frank: A Life in Hiding*. Philadelphia: The Jewish Publication Society, 1988.

McDonough, Yona Zeldis. *Anne Frank*. New York: Henry Holt, 1997.

THE DALAI LAMA

Dalai, Lama. *Answers: Discussions with Western Buddhists*. Ithaca, NY: Snow Lion Publications, 2001.

——. *Freedom in Exile. The Autobiography of the Dalai Lama*. New York: HarperCollins, 1990.

——. *A Human Approach to World Peace*. Boston: Wisdom Publications, 1984.

Hopkins, Jeffrey, and Elizabeth Napper. *Kindness, Clarity, and Insight*. Ithaca, NY: Snow Lion Publications, 1984.

Piburn, Sidney, ed. *The Dalai Lama, A Policy of Kindness: Anthology of Writings*. Ithaca, NY: Snow Lion Publications, 1993.

WANGARI MAATHAI

Maathai, Wangari. *The Green Belt Movement*. New York: Lantern Books, 2004.

Tyler, Patrick E. *The New York Times*. October 8, 2004, section A, page 7; and October 9, 2004, international section, page 9.

AUNG SAN SUU KYI

Clements, Alan. *The Voice of Hope*. New York: Seven Stories Press, 1997.

Ling, Bettina. *Aung San Suu Kyi: Standing for Democracy*. New York: Feminist Press, 1999.

Stewart, Whitney. *Aung San Suu Kyi: Fearless Voice of Burma*. Minneapolis: Lerner Publications, 1997.

PRINCESS DIANA

Adler, Bill, ed. *Diana: A Portrait in Her Own Words*. New York: William Morrow, 1999.

Brennan, Kristine. *Diana, Princess of Wales*. Broomall, PA: Chelsea House, 1998.

FURTHER READING

Clucas, Joan Graff. Introduction by Arthur M. Schlesinger, Jr. *Mother Teresa.* Philadelphia: Chelsea House, 1988.

Dils, Tracey E. *Mother Teresa.* Philadelphia: Chelsea House, 2000.

Emerson, Ralph Waldo. "War" speech. Boston, MA: American Peace Society, 1838. (Internet)

Goldberg, Jake. *The Rebel Behind Relativity.* Danbury, CT: FranklinWatts, 1996.

Keene, Anne T. *Peacemakers: Winners of the Nobel Peace Prize.* New York: Oxford University Press, 1998.

Kennedy, Caroline. *A Patriot's Handbook.* New York: Hyperion, 2003.

Kras, Sara Louise. Introductory Essay by Arthur M. Schlesinger, Jr. *Anwar Sadat.* Philadelphia: Chelsea House, 2003.

Marvis, Barbara J. *Contemporary American Success Stories: Famous People of Hispanic Heritage.* Childs, MD: Mitchell Lane Publishers, 1996.

Schuman, Michael A. *Elie Wiesel: A Voice from the Holocaust.* Hillside, NJ: Enslow Publishers, 1994.

Westra, Hans. Introduction, *A History for Today, Anne Frank.* Amsterdam: Anne Frank House, 1966.

RESOURCES

The Gandhi Institute: (901) 452-2824. www.gandhiinstitute.org

Ralph Bunche: An American Odyssey: PBS documentary on video and DVD

Cesar E. Chavez Foundation: www.cesarechavezfoundation.org

Elie Wiesel Foundation: www.eliewieselfoundation.org

Dalai Lama Foundation: www.dalailamafoundation.org

Schomburg Center for Research in Black Culture at the New York Public Library, archives at: 515 Lenox Avenue at 135 Street, New York, NY, (212) 491-2200

Anne Frank Center (U.S.A.), 38 Crosby Street, fifth floor, New York, NY 10013, www.annefrank.com

Anne Frank Huis (Amsterdam), P.O. Box 730, 1000 AS Amsterdam, The Netherlands, www.annefrank.nl

Israeli and Arab children working together: www.seedsofpeace.org

UNICEF: www.unicefusa.org

Note: You can Google "peace organizations" or the individual peacemaker's name for a website address.

INDEX

RALPH WALDO EMERSON ❧ MAHATMA GANDHI ❧ ALBERT EINSTEIN ❧ ELEANOR ROOSEVELT ❧ RALPH BUNCHE ❧ MOTHER TERESA ❧ JOHN FITZGERALD KENNEDY ❧ ANWAR EL-SADAT ❧ CESAR CHAVEZ ❧ ELIE WIESEL ❧ MARTIN LUTHER KING, JR. ❧ ANNE FRANK ❧ THE DALAI LAMA ❧ WANGARI MAATHAI ❧ AUNG SAN SUU KYI ❧ PRINCESS DIANA ❧ RALPH WALDO EMERSON ❧ MAHATMA GANDHI ❧ ALBERT EINSTEIN ❧ ELEANOR ROOSEVELT ❧ RALPH BUNCHE ❧ MOTHER TERESA ❧ JOHN FITZGERALD KENNEDY ❧ ANWAR EL-SADAT ❧ CESAR CHAVEZ ❧ ELIE WIESEL ❧ MARTIN LUTHER KING, JR. ❧ ANNE FRANK ❧ THE DALAI LAMA ❧ WANGARI MAATHAI ❧ AUNG SAN SUU KYI ❧ PRINCESS DIANA ❧ RALPH WALDO EMERSON ❧ MAHATMA GANDHI ❧ ALBERT EINSTEIN ❧ ELEANOR ROOSEVELT ❧ RALPH BUNCHE ❧ MOTHER TERESA ❧ JOHN FITZGERALD KENNEDY ❧ ANWAR EL-SADAT ❧ CESAR CHAVEZ ❧ ELIE WIESEL ❧ MARTIN LUTHER KING, JR. ❧ ANNE FRANK ❧ THE DALAI LAMA ❧ WANGARI MAATHAI ❧ AUNG SAN SUU KYI ❧ PRINCESS DIANA ❧ RALPH WALDO EMERSON ❧ MAHATMA GANDHI ❧ ALBERT EINSTEIN ❧ ELEANOR ROOSEVELT ❧ RALPH BUNCHE ❧ MOTHER TERESA ❧ JOHN FITZGERALD KENNEDY ❧

RALPH WALDO EMERSON ❧ MAHATMA
ROOSEVELT ❧ RALPH BUNCHE ❧ MOTHER T
EL-SADAT ❧ CESAR CHAVEZ ❧ ELIE
❧ ANNE FRANK ❧ THE DALAI LAMA ❧ V
PRINCESS DIANA ❧ RALPH WALDO EMERS
❧ ELEANOR ROOSEVELT ❧ RALPH BUNC
KENNEDY ❧ ANWAR EL-SADAT ❧ CESAR
KING, JR. ❧ ANNE FRANK ❧ THE DALAI LAI
❧ PRINCESS DIANA ❧ RALPH WALDO EMER
❧ ELEANOR ROOSEVELT ❧ RALPH BUNC
KENNEDY ❧ ANWAR EL-SADAT ❧ CESAR
KING, JR. ❧ ANNE FRANK ❧ THE DALAI LA
❧ PRINCESS DIANA ❧ RALPH WALDO EMER
❧ ELEANOR ROOSEVELT ❧ RALPH BUNC
KENNEDY ❧ ANWAR EL-SADAT ❧ CESAR
KING, JR. ❧ ANNE FRANK ❧ THE DALAI LA
❧ PRINCESS DIANA ❧ RALPH WALDO EMER
❧ ELEANOR ROOSEVELT ❧ RALPH BUNC
KENNEDY ❧ ANWAR EL-SADAT ❧ CESAR CH
JR. ❧ ANNE FRANK ❧ THE DALAI LAMA ❧
❧ PRINCESS DIANA ❧ RALPH WALDO EMEF
❧ ELEANOR ROOSEVELT ❧ RALPH BUNC
KENNEDY ❧ ANWAR EL-SADAT ❧ CESAR
KING, JR. ❧ ANNE FRANK ❧ THE DALAI LA
❧ PRINCESS DIANA ❧ RALPH WALDO
EINSTEIN ❧ ELEANOR ROOSEVELT ❧ R
FITZGERALD KENNEDY ❧ ANWAR EL-SADA
LUTHER KING, JR. ❧ ANNE FRANK ❧ THI
SAN SUU KYI ❧ PRINCESS DIANA ❧ RAL